A Spark

in the

Darkness

A Spark in the Darkness

Karen Higgs-Faretta

ARCHWAY
PUBLISHING

Archway Publishing books may be ordered through
booksellers or by contacting:

Archway Publishing
1663 Liberty Drive
Bloomington, IN 47403
www.archwaypublishing.com
1-(888)-242-5904

ISBN: 978-1-4808-0217-9 (sc)
ISBN: 978-1-4808-0218-6 (e)

Library of Congress Control Number: 2013914848

Printed in the United States of America

Archway Publishing rev. date: 08/21/13

Table of Contents

Introduction 1

Chapter 1: The Start of My Sparks.................................. 3

Chapter 2: Everybody Can Teach Something 7

Chapter 3: Growing Up in the Seventies 11

Chapter 4: Getting Married in the Eighties.................. 15

Chapter 5: The Joy of Having Children......................... 19

Chapter 6: An Ill Child.. 23

Chapter 7: When Jamie Left.. 31

Chapter 8: Slipping into the Dark Hole......................... 35

Chapter 9: Divorce Happens.. 39

Chapter 10: Waking up Paralyzed 41

Chapter 11: The Sparks Never End................................ 45

Chapter 12: I Found a Spark in Low-Income Living.... 47

Chapter 13: I've Learned A Few Things......................... 49

About The Author 53

Introduction

I WROTE THIS BOOK during a period of my life when I went on a quest for reasons behind all of the dark experiences I had endured—divorcing my husband after our eldest daughter's death, trying to rebuild my life with my youngest daughter, and experiencing a brain aneurysm that left me paralyzed on the left side of my body. Not only did I feel a need to find purpose for myself, I also wanted to encourage other people to view their dark experiences or rough roads as opportunities and to look for their own sparks within themselves. I can't find a single experience in which I wasn't able to find a blessing as the final outcome.

In looking back now, I can say that my daughter's death was my absolute darkest experience. I do believe in a purpose, and I did receive a spark within myself during that time. I hold the belief that life does have a rhyme and reason for every experience—even death. Loss is never easy to accept. However, if one truly grieves and is open to finding peace within, he or she will achieve it.

I spent several years in darkness or murky experiences. However, I found that I was never left without a spark—

hope. It is both a desire to move forward and have a feeling of purpose.

I'm certain that nothing in this world happens by accident. This is a belief, not simply words on paper. Victims choose to be victims. Every person is born with free will. In my opinion, free will provides options for viewing every experience that comes along.

All of my circumstances have led to my own personal growth and an internal peace and feeling of well-being. I think the key to this peace is that I listened to the spark within (my inner voice), and I was able to overcome fear through my dark experiences.

I hope that, after reading this book, you will find that life truly is good. If you find yourself in a dark experience, I hope you will be able to feel your own sparks and find a blessing for yourself—even in your most trying, darkest moments—as I found during my own.

Chapter 1

The Start of My Sparks

I FEEL CERTAIN THAT I was born with a spark inside my soul, as is every person. When I say "spark," I am referring to a deep-rooted feeling or belief that our life on this earth is truly a gift and is meant to be good. Life is not to be trudged through. The spark is simply hope, which is inexplicable. Perhaps some of us simply listen to our inner voice who says that anything is possible. I've always heard a tiny whisper that states that it all truly is possible.

I've had several very dark and traumatic experiences thus far in my life. In looking back at them, I can state that the spark never faded from within. I am not a victim in this life, nor have I ever felt that I was one. My darkest experience was when my oldest daughter died suddenly. I was angry, confused, and terribly sad, but I wasn't a victim. I grew to believe that there must be a reason. When I woke up to find myself paralyzed in a hospital, I didn't feel victimized.

Where does the spark come from? Don't we all wonder about this in our darkness? When did my sparks begin? I always knew that life was to be enjoyed. Then I became a mom. I found out that my firstborn daughter was very ill with a severe heart defect. I prayed for a spark. Fear does that to one. Love can cause darkness. If love is threatened (I loved my daughter very much), it can turn to a black fear at the thought of losing the one you love dearly. In the darkness of fear, a spark is a precious gift to receive. A spark can simply be inner strength along with hope. I determined that when my daughter was ill. I discovered it was true that, if you ask for help, you will receive it.

Through every dark experience, I asked for a spark. I found that there was not a way that I could be a victim of life. A spark received is free. The key is all in the asking. But who gives out the free sparks? Where do they come from? Is it the angels, or is it God? Do they have a magic wand and zap those who ask? Do they walk among us offering sprinkles of joy? Perhaps it doesn't matter, as no person can state for a fact where the sparks come from.

I've often wondered why there is such misery in society. Are there people who are afraid to ask for a spark or help? Are sparks only for a select few people on earth? The only thing I did to gain strength is pray, and someone somehow heard me. I don't know who did. I can only tell you that I was never left without and I never felt alone during my trials. In every single dark experience I faced, a spark was within.

When I was young, I heard in my Episcopalian

church that all any person needs in order to receive is a mustard seed of faith. (I am not preaching religion; I am just stating what I heard as a child in church.) Somehow, all that I listened to about God seemed to sink in and prepare me for future experiences.

My sparks, therefore, began in my childhood. Listening played a large role in receiving. Belief doesn't always come that easily for everyone. I believe that having proof of what I had been told in church has made me a whole person today. I have received the proof.

I suppose that every person can receive a spark after asking for help and then turning around and feeling victimized by the world. Attitude plays a role in happiness. Even in my darkest of black times, I found it helpful to be thankful for a spark, that is, hope.

Chapter 2

Everybody Can Teach Something

WHEN I WAS SIXTEEN years old, I worked behind a locked ward for elderly residents as a certified nursing assistant. A great job, it was my first one with a paycheck and taxes deducted. I met wonderful people I cared for. The residents apparently had psychiatric conditions, but I liked them and enjoyed their company.

I saw a poem on the wall on my first day on the job. The first line read, "Young lady, what do you see when you look at me?" This poem reminded me that I was going to be an old lady someday. I thought I had a large responsibility to offer very good care to the elderly individuals.

These people who were near the end of their lives had much to offer. They still do today because I can still remember most of their names. I am writing about them and having fond memories of what these elderly psychiatric patients taught me about life.

I celebrated one lady's 103rd birthday with her. I helped her to blow out her candles. She was in a wheelchair with a restraint. She had so much spunk that I would find her breaking out of her restraints and walking around her room when she wasn't supposed to be out of her chair. Back then, I wanted to be like that little old lady.

Brushing patients' dentures was part of my job. I washed my first dead body after watching a woman take her last breath. Life is like that. We get older, lose our teeth, and die. That was quite a dose of reality for a sixteen-year-old.

I decided that looks didn't matter. Some of these people had wrinkles, others were in wheelchairs, many wore diapers, and several screamed and cried. The stories that some of these little old people had to tell revealed interesting lives. They had lived through the storms, and they were near their end. They all had victories, too.

One lady smiled all of the time because she could only feel happiness, not anger. She showed me progress in the medical field. I was told that, years before I met her, she would get mad and throw a fit. She eventually had a lobotomy, that is, where part of the brain is cut out where there is anger. I didn't know much about that then, and I still don't know much now. I do know that the medical field does not allow lobotomy as a form of treatment any longer. That must be progress because it didn't sound like a good solution to me. Change is constant. Growth seems inevitable. I am certain that there have been errors in medicine throughout the course of history. Humans are not perfect, and they don't always have the correct answer.

Another lady was always laughing and smiling, but she hadn't had a lobotomy. She never appeared to be negative, and she didn't bring down others with insults. She was in a perpetually good mood. I was curious as to why this was. I tried to get to know her better.

When I asked her about her family, I learned she was from Germany. She talked very briefly about the Hitler era. She did not talk much of it because it was an ugly subject for her. I never knew much about history, so I was never clear if her family members had been in the gas chambers. Perhaps that was why she did not want to talk much. I didn't ask her. I concluded from her that a good attitude would lead to a happy life.

I don't think that a person must be famous or do great things in the world in order to make an impact on others' lives or to teach something. I learned this very early in my own life from a ward of elderly people.

I also discovered early on that even a former felon has something to offer to others. When my son got hurt from falling off his bike, a former felon, our neighbor, comforted him. I am not saying that every former criminal ought to be invited in for supper, but our neighbor turned out to have many good qualities as a human being. I used my instincts when I befriended him. Because we lived close to each other, it was better to be neighborly rather than live in fear of a felon. If he were a threat to society, then he wouldn't have been my neighbor. It turned out to be a good experience for my impressionable son.

My son liked this felon, but this felon was also a human being with a name. My son enjoyed having guy talks with him once he got to know him. I didn't really know how I felt about my little boy being friends with a felon. So I watched very closely and kept my phone with me at all times in case I needed to call the police for any reason, but I did not need to. This human being with a name told my son all about prison life. They would be sitting outside, and this man did a boy a favor by telling him of his own prison experience. I was glad we made friends with him. That man may have scared my son straight with his honesty. One never knows what gifts can be received through a simple conversation or making a new friend.

Chapter 3

Growing Up in the Seventies

I LOVED GROWING UP in the seventies, the sex, drugs, and rock 'n' roll era. I proudly wore my jersey making my claim to that when I was a teenager. It was such a colorful era. It was bright and bold. I think the seventies were a step up from the sixties. Doesn't every generation move up a notch from the previous one? I like to think that we are all evolving and growing in order to reach our potential as a human race. It also seems to me that every generation can learn from its previous cohorts and vice versa. Listening to each other is beneficial. I never wanted my children to live the teen years as I did. It was fun; however, it was a very wild era.

The dark side of the seventies was that drinking and drugs were very much the norm for many. Suicide was not unheard of. Dysfunction was normal. I myself lost many friends to drinking and driving. It was not common to see individuals who celebrated themselves or expressed their emotions in a healthy way. It seemed to be an era in which everyone silently asked, *what are we supposed to be doing here?* There really weren't any guidelines established except for the spiritual directives that have always been around. The spark for me growing up in the seventies was that I taught my own children to think for themselves and to value their own instincts, feel their own emotions, and celebrate themselves.

I faced several traumatic events in my early childhood. Everyone has faced trauma in one way or another. Life really isn't smooth sailing. Drama, loss, and pain, along with triumph and joy, fills it. How would anyone develop a personality if every single day were the same? I believe that my past experiences gave me something to draw from. Dysfunction is not a problem in my mind because abnormality fills the world. It's good to be able to handle myself with imperfect people who are growing at their own pace.

Simple childhood events along with major trauma such as our home being robbed and a few fires in our neighborhood, including one that took the lives of three children, definitely filled my early years. Anyone could read the news and see all of the terrible things going on in the world or focus on the spark. We have much to gain by finding the spark in every situation and making it good.

There was less divorce in the seventies. There was some; however, the trend was to stay married. That in itself was a sense of security to me. We didn't have to deal with our parents' boyfriends and girlfriends nor multiple partners coming and going. I knew where I came from and who my family was. That's not necessarily right or wrong; it is simply the way it was for many of us. I'm not making a judgment.

The women's lib movement hit during the seventies. My mom did find her way to paving her own career in the workforce. Change for many does not come easily, but it is inevitable. It was difficult for my dad because he was raised in England by a mother who stayed home and raised her family. His mom did not work outside of the family; neither did my mom's mom. The movement was a result of dissatisfaction and restlessness. There was a desire to have more from life. Change seems to creep up on society, and not everyone is receptive to change.

My teenage years were of a different flavor. There were the separate social groups. We as teenagers were looking for our identities. Doesn't every teenager look for his or her distinctiveness? There are so many ways to obtain it. I myself went after my identity by partying and rebelling. Some became scholarly or got into sports. There was a sense of separation with the social status that one held. Perhaps it takes some a lifetime to fully know oneself. Doesn't every generation have the gap amongst their parents and teenagers? Embracing diversity and clear communication might be the bridge to the space.

I would never deny that I had fun during my teenage years. There was always a party to go to. There was plenty of drinking and a great social life. At that time, school was not a priority. It takes some of us a little more time to bloom than others. Growth is good for society. It brings some change.

I have noticed that many adults from my generation appear to be stuck at an emotional teenage level. Drinking at that age seems to stunt emotional growth. The spark I see today is that so many from the generation below me place a high emphasis on living life to the fullest. Education has become a priority. Did that generation learn from ours? I know that I outgrew my teenage years long ago.

The seventies were grand. It's a piece of history. I'm sure every person who grew up in that era has a separate point of view. I loved it.

Chapter 4

Getting Married in the Eighties

BACK WHEN I WAS in high school, many people had a true love. The logical thing to do was to get married. I know for myself that I didn't put a lot of thought into the union of marriage. Honestly, I didn't know that I was supposed to. There wasn't a lot of information at that time about the development of relationships or what it took to make a marriage last. I had my parents and grandparents to use as my role models. It looked easy to maintain a marriage. It seemed to me that couples simply needed to accept the other person for who he or she was and work together for life. I now know that a couple must be compatible. They should find out prior to getting married if they have the same long-term goals.

I met my future husband when I was in the sixth grade. We started dating when we were seventeen years old. We got together during a costume party. There wasn't actually formal dating or courting for us. It was not the most glamorous of starts.

We did become inseparable all throughout high school. We shared many interesting times together, like traveling to England with each other and getting arrested while a riot broke out at a concert. It was a wild relationship before we got married. There are many good and bad memories.

After we graduated in June 1981, we planned to get married precisely three years later We chose, at first, to wait an appropriate amount of time , after we graduated from high school before getting married.. There are those few people who can marry their high school sweethearts and make it last for life. Then there are those of us who can't. I think many people would like a lifetime marriage. I just assumed I would have one.

In August 1983, I got pregnant with our first daughter when both of us were twenty-one. I had always questioned if premarital sex was right or wrong. On one hand, it is good to know your partner at an intimate level. The other point, seemingly old fashioned, is that one should be a virgin according to spiritual guidelines. At that time, I'm not sure how many people put thought into premarital sex. Whether it was right or wrong, it turned out to be very exciting to start a family.

It is amazing how fast a wedding can be put together. Our baby was due in April 1984. We started our to-do list. First, we were to plan the wedding for December 3, 1983. I didn't need an extravagant ceremony. We were simply married in a little red church on top of a hill in the town I grew up in. I bought my wedding dress from a mall for $150. It was originally supposed to be sold as a prom dress. I wore my mother's veil. I had my values of what I thought should happen for my wedding day. I didn't hold the belief that money could buy a happy marriage. Simple was fine. In my mind, the point of getting married was because we loved each other and wanted to share our lives together. The family was on its way already. We decided to have a candlelit evening wedding. It did turn out to be a great wedding day in my mind. It was not a perfect day, but I didn't expect it to be a fairy-tale wedding.

I'm glad that I did get married and I could start a family at a young age. Things don't always turn out the way a person would like them to; however, I would not have missed the experience of getting married in the eighties.

Chapter 5

The Joy of Having Children

I WAS FIVE MONTHS pregnant when I got married. We had four months to get ready for our baby. Is anybody really ready for parenthood? One can read plenty of books on child rearing; however, every child is unique. There isn't a direct path to take to raise a child. I guess one can only play it by ear and use his or her instincts.

My husband and I were both twenty-one, newly married, and heading into parenthood. We were living in a rented house. The heat was expensive because it was electric. We both had to work in order to have a roof over our heads. Neither one of us was making a large wage, yet we somehow managed to budget our money. We had moved straight from our parents' homes and didn't have experience with living on our own. We learned quickly. It was an exciting time. The thought of starting out and making a good home for our baby left me feeling ecstatic.

Easter 1984 was just around the corner. I was working in an office, and when I left work on Thursday, April 20, I was certain I would be back on Monday morning. I wished my coworkers a happy Easter as I walked out the door.

On Easter Sunday, I found out exactly what the meaning of Easter meant. It was the joy that comes after the chaos. I am referring to the chaos of throwing a wedding together in a few months, finding a place to call home, and adjusting to marriage. It is chaotic to have so many changes in one's life.

Our oldest daughter, Jamie Rose, was born on April 22, 1984. The pure joy came when, after six pushes during labor, I laid eyes on a blonde little angel, our daughter. It is hard to describe the awe I felt when meeting a miracle. The sense of responsibility that comes with a newborn baby was overwhelming.

She was pronounced a healthy baby girl, but a couple months later, we found out that she was very ill as she was born with a severe heart defect. The above words by Helen Keller gave me the strength I needed to be able to watch my oldest daughter go through what she needed to in her short life. *Character cannot be developed in ease and quiet. Only through experiences of trial and suffering can the soul be strengthened, vision cleared, ambition inspired, and success achieved.*

I did not take motherhood and its responsibilities lightly. There were fears that also came along with having a newborn child. I wondered if we would serve this child well as parents and if we had the ability to fully care for her and protect her. Protecting a child from everything that could cause her harm, is that possible for any parent to do? I later found out that it is not something that any of us has the ability to do. I discovered that, as a parent, the greatest gift I could give to my child was my heart.

I had a sinking feeling in the pit of my spirit for many months before I had our daughter. I couldn't shake the feeling of dread. I didn't have a rational explanation for my sense. I discovered that it is best not to have an explanation for everything. Some things in life are best to be unknown. The future proved to be held with many surprises. Some surprises come with darkness. Along with the dark is a spark of light.

We had just started our new life. We had everything that we needed as a small family. We loved our daughter, we were able to care and provide for her, and life was good indeed. We discovered that we were capable. Then our family went right back into the joys of having children. During the next few months, I got pregnant with our second child. We were delighted to hear the good news. Our next baby would be due in April 1985, making them one year apart. It was time to start preparing for our growing family.

Some people viewed us as crazy because medical bills from our oldest daughter swamped us and now we had another child on the way. It is true that if one has faith, then nothing is impossible. Somehow, the bills get paid, and life has a way of working itself out.

On April 28, 1985, our dark-haired, olive-skinned

daughter was born. I was thrilled to have another girl. Motherhood came naturally to me, and I loved it. Joy and parenthood go together in my mind.

The joy of another child could not be dimmed. It was a fact that our oldest daughter was not able to walk yet due to her weakness. We had more darkness to go through yet; however, we had our two beautiful girls with us, at least for that particular moment. I was learning to take life one moment at a time already.

There we were at the age of twenty-two years old, married with two young girls and very little life experiences under our belts. We did find that we had a love-filled household. I found that having children was a joy like no other. Our families fell in love too during that time.

Later in my life, at the age of thirty-eight, I did get another surprise after I got divorced. I had a son in December 2000. I was once again thrilled. I wasn't married; however, children add so much to life. I love having my children in my existence, and I adore being a mom through the good and dark times.

Chapter 6

An Ill Child

Character cannot be developed in ease and quiet. Only through experiences of trial and suffering can the soul be strengthened, vision cleared, ambition inspired, and success achieved.

Helen Keller

JAMIE ROSE WAS BORN with five major heart defects. We learned of this after her pediatrician found spots on her lungs. We later found out that the blood from her heart pounding through caused the spots. It was initially thought that she might have cystic fibrosis. Because she was having trouble breathing, her physician ordered an x-ray to determine what was wrong.

Jamie was only two months old. I could watch how hard she worked to push the air in and out. It is called labored breathing. We had fallen in love with her already. She was a part of her community and family.

I, along with my sister-in-law, took Jamie to have an

x-ray. When it was completed and I saw the technician's face, I knew that Jamie was in deep trouble. The technician didn't say a word. She couldn't hide her emotions from me. It was apparent with the upcoming news that our pediatrician would give us.

Jamie got the x-ray on a Friday. We would have to wait for the results until Monday morning. It was a very long, emotion-filled weekend. We had no news to give to our families. We only knew for certain that Jamie Rose had something wrong with her.

It is hard to keep a quiet mind in times of uncertainty. I went to church that Sunday. I learned to rely on faith that day. I trusted in a faith that God was in charge of this world and a faith that would quiet the fear I had been feeling since that Friday. I hoped for a master plan that would spare my daughter from pain.

I discovered that weekend that there isn't a person in the world who can tangibly help a terrified mom. The only thing I could do that weekend was to pray, sit, and feel all my fear emerging. No one could have offered any words that would have helped ease my anxiety. The fact of the matter was that nobody had an answer as to what was going to become of my daughter. It was the worst unknown I had to live with.

Monday morning arrived. Her pediatrician called and said he was referring us to Children's Hospital. I could feel the sinking feeling to my core. It had to be more than a simple infection, or he would have given her antibiotics. He didn't have an answer. More waiting was to come until we could get to the specialist. Waiting for others to determine our daughter's fate meant having faith in a holy outcome. Everyone, I think, might want to plan his or her own outcome. But how much control does any of us really have?

We were able to get an appointment with a cardiologist. The lung specialist was out of town. The doctor we saw immediately put us to ease. He was a kindly, older man who specialized in children with heart defects. He appeared to have much experience and confidence. We were a young couple who loved our daughter. We wanted good news from him. Surely he must have been a grandfather himself. It was easy to trust him with our baby because he cared.

At this point, I only wanted to grab the cardiologist and convince him how important our daughter was to us and how much we loved her. I'm sure he knew, but he must have also known that, as a physician, he was not God and he could only do what technology and his skills would allow him to do for her.

When our daughter was older, I called this doctor at his home because Jamie appeared to be dying before my eyes. She didn't look or sound right. This cardiologist drove to our home on his time off and checked on our daughter. I determined that this man had passion. He loved our daughter, too. It turned out to be pneumonia that day. During her life, she had several bouts of it. Fluid would fill her lungs, making her breathing harder.

On that first visit, they hooked up our baby to a monitor, and we could hear the echo of her heart swooshing through the office. The cardiologist took one listen and gave us the news. Jamie had transposition of the greater arteries. I didn't know anything about the heart muscle. Physicians speak their own language I had discovered. I speak in laymen's terms and did not, nor do not have the understanding of technical terminology. I knew about emotions and the fact that I needed to comfort my baby as she would need a heart surgery to repair her arteries. I remember thinking to myself, *Good. The doctor can fix her heart.* I tried to make this ordeal uncomplicated. But it was not straightforward. It was very serious.

We were introduced to a heart surgeon. I didn't feel at ease with anything by this point. We were in a big city hospital with people we didn't know, men and women who were to be in charge of our daughter's life. Trust does not come that easy.

The surgeon who was to hold our daughter's heart proved to be very skilled. We eventually did trust him, along with the entire medical team. These people at Children's Hospital became a big part of our lives and vice versa. It would be impossible to not form a bond with the people who worked so hard to fix our child. It couldn't have been easy for them to watch a parent in torment.

We met other parents who also had children born with heart defects. One tends to form relationships easily when in the same boat. We did form a free support group for parents in our community called "The Little Hearts," a place where parents of children facing heart surgery could come together in safety to share with each other. Not many wanted to belong to this group.

We were able to laugh, cry, be angry, and feel afraid. We were to stay together for a short amount of time. Each of us understood the others. When one of us had an outburst of anger that may have appeared odd to an onlooker, we didn't judge. A parent with an ill child understands that being appropriate at all times every day does not occur. I am referring to the moments when agitation or annoyance rises up and gets thrown at an innocent bystander. I'm sorry to state that, when a parent receives news that his or her child needs yet another heart surgery, he or she needs an outlet that will help him or her to maintain his or her sanity. This group did this for us. This small group was not a pity party meeting in any way. It was an honest group of individuals who formed a bond of understanding.

The medical team who were in care of our children were also simply human. We all knew that none of us had anybody to blame, including the people trying to fix our kids. We also knew that we wanted to have a cure from them. A parent with an ill child is grateful for an ounce of hope that anyone could give him or her. At times, I wanted to hear from our daughter's doctor that he was indeed going to fix her so she could have a normal life like the healthy kids in the world.

But our daughter wasn't healthy. She had blue fingertips, and she was very thin. She had to work harder at life than a healthy child. The other kids at Children's Hospital were not healthy either, or they would not have been there. They were lovable, beautiful, and very special.

I can tell you that every parent wants to hear his or her child's doctor confidently say, "I promise I can cure your child." When the doctor has only the truth to offer, anger arises. It tends to get misplaced when a parent grasps at straws of hope. Our little group remained together for only a short period of time because there wasn't a lot of knowledge about children being born with heart defects in 1985. More research needed to be done on the heart muscle.

At that time, the only thing I knew was that I loved my daughter. She was a part of my husband and me. I had no idea how to fix a broken heart. A variety of people—the medical profession who were trained to fix children at this big hospital—surrounded us. We chose to put our baby in their hands in the hopes that they cared. We had just met them, and as it turned out, they did have concern. They truly appeared to have a passion for helping children.

It seemed as if God gave to us when we needed to be provided for. Should we prepare to bury our daughter? Should we be hopeful that they would fix her heart? I decided to feel the way I felt. I felt terrified either way. I wanted to run away, come back, and have everything be all right in the world. But I stayed put.

At the age of two months, our baby was to have her first minor heart surgery at Children's Hospital. I was pregnant at that time. A medical team was in place. Their job was to decide what was best for our daughter. We were unable to determine what was best for her. We didn't have the knowledge. We were forced to trust these people we had just met with her life.

Before her first surgery, the staff prepared us for the intensive care unit. They informed us that our child would have many different tubes in her body. They said she might appear to be blue due to a lack of oxygen. They were preparing us for the horror any parent would face when his or her child is in intensive care.

The day came for Jamie's first heart surgery. It was very difficult to watch the medical team wheel our child through the big surgery doors and stay in a waiting room with friends and family. Other scared people sat and waited with us for several hours. It helped to reach out to them and even to laugh during the long wait. We learned to amuse ourselves during surgery. There were ridiculous times when someone would have a fit of laughter. We laughed because it eased the tension in the waiting room. Laughter for many is truly the best medicine.

Finally, the heart surgeon walked into the waiting area. He had a look of relief on his face. By this time I had learned to watch people very closely so I could monitor their reactions, and their body language, along with their facial expression .I watched closely so that I could get a clear picture or idea as to what was going to happen next. The moment arrived when the surgeon came to tell us the latest news.. A nurse followed after the surgeon. They informed us that the surgery went well. Her heart wasn't completely fixed yet. Her heart needed a total repair in order for her to survive. Jamie essentially got a band aid for her heart. It would get her through for a while until the major heart repair could be done, which would need to wait until she was older and able to withstand the long surgery. We could go into the intensive care unit and see our daughter.

There is not a way that a parent can prepare themselves for seeing their child lying in the intensive care unit with tubes coming out of their body. Although the staff had tried to prepare us for the way Jamie would look, they didn't. At the first look at your child lying in the hospital bed, you have two options; you can fall emotionally apart or you can fake it, being strong and brave. I faked it! I wasn't brave and I didn't feel strong nor did I truly trust.

Jamie's health would improve, and then it would deteriorate. She would have periods of pneumonia. She was on medication. She, along with us, would have good and bad days. Her good days were really great days. Triumph filled them. Taking her first steps in the grass moved her and us emotionally. They were her accomplishments.

My oldest daughter taught me many things. Even though her bad days were rough on all of us, I wouldn't have missed out on her life. I learned to live in the moment and to be grateful for it. Tiny steps are better than not taking any at all. Taking a risk is better than being idle or living in fear. A smile can help anyone any at any time or anywhere.

When Jamie left us all, we were devastated, but in her honor, we carried on bravely as best as we could.

Chapter 7

When Jamie Left

THE LAST TIME I saw Jamie Rose, it was an early Saturday morning. She held her Raggedy Ann doll. I went over and kissed her good-bye. She cupped my face in her hands and said, "I love you, Mommy." I said, "I love you back." That was the last time I saw Jamie Rose alive.

On September 11, 1988, Grandparent's Day, I left for my job down the road from where we lived. I wasn't planning to come home right after work. I went to a friend's house after my shift was completed to help with her daughter's sixteenth birthday party.

I got home at about midnight. It was my usual nightly routine to go into my daughters' room and kiss them good night. I walked in and went to kiss Jamie on her forehead and found that it was ice cold. I screamed for my husband. Waves of shock and disbelief ran through my body. Joe grabbed Jamie's body and brought her into the living room, and he hovered over her while screaming. I am sorry to say that this is reality.

I ran to the phone and called 911. I then called our neighbor, and she came over and tried to resuscitate her. My other daughter, Mandy, woke up. Jamie and Mandy were three and four years old at this time. I grabbed her, ran outside, and waited for the ambulance to arrive. Mandy started screaming that Jamie was only sleeping. When the ambulance arrived, I screamed to them that they were too late. Jamie had died before I got home. My husband got into the ambulance with Jamie and the medical team. My neighbor took Mandy back to her house. I guess I, then got into my car and drove to the hospital with my guardian angel with me and screaming to myself: Jamie is dead."

I MUST HAVE HAD a guardian angel driving with me because I don't believe I would have been coherent enough to drive myself to the hospital otherwise. That night at the hospital, we all said good-bye to sweet Jamie Rose. It was devastating. It was determined that she went into heart failure.

I THINK JAMIE MAY have known that she was going to die. A month before she died, Jamie woke up, and she was beaming. She was so excited. She ran up to me.

"I saw Grandpa Faretta last night."

I knew he had died a year earlier. "What do you mean?"

She said, "He said he has lots of presents for me in heaven."

I was stunned. Emotionally, I shut down. I didn't want to know. Since my daughter had been born, I had periodically seen pictures of her lying in a coffin in my mind. It had always been an unbearable thought or image. It was terrifying to say the least.

The Saturday Jamie died was not the last time I felt Jamie. I can't prove it. I believe that, since she died, I have been able to feel her presence or spirit. I am not referring to a ghost. I have heard many other people speak of feeling a departed loved one. I am not denying that she died. I am only making the claim that I have felt my departed daughter at different times. I don't know why.

This experience shaped my adult life. I have never forgotten my daughter. I have spent my life living with the sorrow of a missing piece of myself. I did choose to believe in a purpose for her life and death. I also decided to go on living my own life. It has not been without sadness and longing.

I have concluded that, in this case, love really does hurt. I would not have missed out on her short life. In truth, loss is very painful. It is hard to understand death and the reason it exists. It is hard to believe that God is always good when one loses a person that he or she loves so deeply. We all love the people in our lives deeply. We all question life and death.

I do believe that God is good and there is a reason for my daughter's passing. The night she died was so very painful, and I live with it along with my sparks.

Jamie Rose lived to be four years old. In her short

time on this earth, my daughter lived longer than was predicted with her severe heart defect. She learned how to swim, she rode her pink bike with training wheels, she played in our sandbox, she made many friends, she was loved very much, her family adored her, she laughed a lot, she baked cookies with her sister, and she smiled a lot. Other than time, I don't think that a mom could ask more for her daughter.

After Jamie died, we did choose to go on with life. I'm certain that life is for the living. To try to make some sense out of her death, many people in our family participated in fundraisers to benefit the National Heart Foundation. My dad even met a little girl in Haiti who needed a heart surgery. She was a little older than Jamie was. The Haitian girl was brought to America and received her operation. She survived. I have since met a young boy in my son's playgroup (I had another child at the age of thirty-eight) with the same condition as Jamie. This boy was not blue; he was not breathing hard. He was laughing and running during this playgroup.

I am happy to say that, when it comes to progress of the heart, we have come a long way!

Chapter 8

Slipping into the Dark Hole

W E HELD THE FUNERAL for my daughter on September 13, 1988. I don't think I would consider myself to be human if I didn't admit to slipping into the deep hole of depression after she died. But I call it a situational depression where the situation of losing my daughter caused my despair. I had never been in such a dark place before.

The sadness was so overwhelming. A spark was always with me during this time. I now know that this is part of the grieving process. At times, it felt like this was an unending emotional roller-coaster ride. It took at least a year to come to terms with the reality of this loss. The grief process does not have a time frame. We cannot set a deadline for healing from such a loss. I had often wondered if a parent actually ever would get over losing his or her child. And I didn't just lose my daughter. I lost my marriage, home, and lifestyle. I lost all my dreams. My life was never to be the same.

It is hard to describe the ache of loss. Anger comes along with the sorrow. The spark of hope held me up during the flatline zone, the place of dullness and lifelessness. During this phase, I had to look for reasons to keep moving onward. The other option was to sink further into the pit. I chose to keep my thoughts from drifting into despair. I had Mandy, my future son that arrived years later, my son-in-law, and granddaughter to think of.

Terror came with this process. At times, I would be up in the middle of the night when my emotions would start to surface and my thoughts would wonder into the unknown. My heart would race, my chest would hurt, and fear would fill me. I found only one way to get through these panic attacks, to simply embrace the fear and feel it.

After our daughter died, my husband and I separated. I was responsible for Mandy, and in the middle of the night when fear came, I found my courage. I had fears about the afterlife. I had been told about heaven in church. I know the Christian teachings. I needed proof. Where exactly is heaven? Was my daughter all right there? Could she see me? I had so many questions. There was such a feeling of not having the ability to control my daughter's fate. Death is not only painful to the living; it can also be very frightening.

This dark hole felt like hell. I couldn't accept my daughter leaving without asking questions. The emotions in the middle of the night were all part of the release process that eventually led me to accept loss and change.

I didn't choose to medicate my overwhelming feelings. I simply decided to feel every painful emotion.

On some days, it felt as if there were not an end to the bottomless pit. I would then pray for guidance. Every single time I asked for help, I received a spark from somewhere or someone. I could call it a sign or hope. It gave me strength to keep going.

During this time and change in my life, I got a job at a treatment center and worked with people who were suffering with depression and addictions. I needed a job that offered more money so I could support Mandy and me because we were on our own. Our family had gone from the four of us and our dog to just Mandy and me. The spark was that I was able to support us, and I found a small one-bedroom apartment to live in.

The dark side of this job was that depressed people, including myself, were everywhere. Same seemed to attract same. I am referring to healing. It was a reflection of people together. I learned a lot working with this wide variety of people. I had the opportunity to read much good information from the library of books that the facility offered. I was paid to give emotional support to others. I also helped myself while assisting them. I believe that the only way to get through a traumatic event is to face it head-on.

Facing it in my mind means feeling it. Reality can't be changed; however, it can be accepted and grieved. I could not change the fact that my daughter had died. I could not have concrete answers to the reasons. But I could feel my sorrow of loss, build a life with my living daughter, and keep moving forward with my sadness.

I have made pit stops in the hole periodically since my daughter died. I have come to believe that life is always changing, people leave our lives, and there will be sorrow when this happens. I do know that I can pull myself out of the hole by simply feeling my way out of it. I am speaking of emotionally feeling. I give myself confidence with my belief system.

Chapter 9

Divorce Happens

I WAS TWENTY-FIVE YEARS old. I had married at the age of twenty-one. I intended to be married for the rest of my life. My husband and I separated two months after Jamie died. It is not uncommon for couples to part. Grieving can be done in so many ways. It is such an individual process. It could be that losing a child for both of the parents may force them to face each other and their own pain. Not every couple can withstand that agony together. Staying together can constantly remind them of the love they lost. It can be a thorn poking at your open wound, and it is sometimes easier to get rid of that painful thorn and move on to start a fresh life.

The ending of a marriage can also be a constant pain that one must live with, a reminder of what might have been. At times, it has felt to me like an unfair waste of an experience. In my mind, loss can make people cherish life more and each other.

It is amazing to me how fast the union of marriage

can be abolished. The day I got divorced, it took a total of ten minutes in court. How sad that has always seemed to me. I had put much thought into the notion of divorce. What does it do to kids? Everyone must learn to cope with other people in his or her child's life once the divorce is complete. It is blended families. So much is to be considered when divorce occurs.

Trust has played a large part in my divorce. Letting go of control of all outcomes helped me get through my own divorce. It wasn't always easy because ex-spouses add new people to their lives. I had hoped that I taught my daughter to trust her instincts so she could be a good judge of newcomers' characters. I felt I could trust my daughter to keep herself safe with any new people in her life. That could simply be good old-fashioned street smarts. One benefit of divorce is that they do get used to having a wider variety of people in their lives, leading to children being able to handle themselves in their own lives.

I am not against or for divorce. It just happens sometimes. It is another grieving process that one must go through. It is change.

Chapter 10

Waking up Paralyzed

I WAS A HAPPY single mom and working full-time by 1994. I had gotten back on my feet after my previous dark experiences. Then I was down again. On November 25, 1994, the day after Thanksgiving, I was at work by seven thirty that morning. There was nothing out of the ordinary that day. Ten days later, I woke up in a hospital, and the left side of my body was paralyzed, my right eye was closed shut, and half of my hair was shaved off my head. I was alive though.

Before waking up paralyzed, I was at work, on a call with a client, when the temples of my head started to hurt like I had never felt before. I ended the phone call, went into another room, and lay down. I didn't think it was serious at all. I went and locked myself in the bathroom to try to outrun the pain in my head or possibly find relief. Eventually, the paramedics were called to take me to the local hospital. It was first thought that I was having a migraine headache. My coworker who had come with me told the hospital staff that I had never complained of migraines previously. The doctor then ordered a CT scan to be done on me. I was given pain medication, but I got no relief from the pain.

The CT scan showed an aneurysm at the base of my brain. I was then flown in the Flight for Life helicopter to a bigger hospital. A very qualified brain surgeon would perform the surgery at the base of my brain. The base of the brain is, I was told, a very tricky area for surgery. The surgery was scheduled for ten days after my arrival because my brain had swelled up.

Prayers went out for me while I waited for surgery. There is something to be said for the power of prayer. My coworkers had a prayer service at work, and they put me on a prayer chain. They said prayers for my survival of the upcoming surgery that I faced.

December 6, 1994, was the day to have brain surgery. The outcome offered me a 40 percent chance of survival. I was told that, if I were in the 40 percent, then I had a 60 percent chance of having other impairments. I was heavily medicated at that time. I didn't really comprehend all that I was told, nor did I face my own mortality. I wasn't alert enough to actually be afraid of the outcome or what was really going on. I was, however, offered last rights by the hospital Chaplin. I did not want last rights and wanted to live.

I woke up in a hospital room, and I was paralyzed. That is an unbelievable way to wake up. It was too much for me to comprehend. Reality crept in slowly for me during my hospital stay. I cried a lot when I realized what had happened to my life. I was offered medication to curb my tears; however, I felt like I would be better off to just release my emotions. I found out that it is very hard on some people to watch another releasing his or her emotions because strong feelings can hurt others as well.

The medical staff was more than qualified to help me with my rehabilitation process to get me walking again. It was my personal life challenge to do so. I turned physical therapy into a fun time. I sang songs, laughed, and worked hard to walk. I always had family and friends coming into the hospital to visit and offer their support during my hospital stay. I would not have gotten through this experience without all of the prayers and support of others.

The therapies I received paid off. I walked out of the hospital with Mandy's and her dad's assistance and I felt grateful to be alive that day. Life had once again changed. It takes time to adjust to it. I did know by that point that, if I chose to make that a positive experience, then it would be.

Because I have a left side weakness, I have never walked as I did prior to my paralysis. I discovered from that experience that I am not my body. I could love myself in my ugliest of moments. That is true commitment to oneself.

I don't know exactly how prayers are answered, and I don't know why they are responded to. I do know that life is still a mystery.

Chapter 11

The Sparks Never End

I STARTED WRITING THIS book in 1996. It was just a draft. I thought it was complete, but I was mistaken. I later found that, after getting evicted, going bankrupt, moving several times, getting evicted again, getting fired, getting pregnant with my healthy son, becoming a mother-in-law, and becoming a grandmother, I needed more experience in order to complete it.

After Jamie died, I bought a poster with the words of Helen Keller. It said "Life Is a Daring Adventure or Nothing." I still have that poster in a frame. I have taken it with me every new place I have ever lived. I have lived in many new places for several reasons. I did briefly visit the dark hole at some point. The older I get, the easier it is to skip out of the hole. It must be a benefit of getting older. In my mind, life gets easier.

Many changes have taken place since my early dark experiences. I will still make the claim that life is indeed good and I still won't trudge through it. I had my only son in 2000. I did not marry his father. We did develop a loving friendship though we were not in love as a couple would be if they had married. I am sad to say that our son witnessed his father take his last breath. Eleven years old is quite young to go through such a traumatic experience. I will state that my son's dad had joy in his life before he left at the age of fifty-seven. I discovered that children also are given sparks to help them move forward with their own lives after loss.

I do know that children have many questions about death. They have their own emotional outburst at the unfairness of it. I have to admit that, though I've been on my own quest for answers, I still don't have them all. I do know that somehow the right words come out of my own mouth when I try to explain to my own son why his father died. I have prayed for guidance.

I can honor my son's dad by helping our son go into manhood with his own courage. I have watched my son smile again through his pain. I see how he is getting his own colors as a human being.

Chapter 12

I Found a Spark in Low-Income Living

A FEW TIMES, I have needed to live in subsidized low-income housing projects. It means that if you have a low income, there is a place to live in which your income level calculates your rent. Many people benefit from this type of housing. But a stigma can go with living in a low-income housing project. It may not matter if one is working with a low wage, raising his or her children, and contributing to his or her community. Some people frown on subsidized living. I can only speak for myself and say I have always found a spark wherever I have lived. I believe that if you have a roof over your head, then you are blessed. It really does not matter what others think.

I lived in two low-income apartment complexes with Mandy after my divorce. I was working full-time in both places. The apartments I rented were both very nice places to call home for a period of needed time. It is good to know that there is a place to live for anyone regardless of how much his or her paycheck is.

I once again needed a place for my son and I to live after his dad and I went our separate ways. This time, I needed to rent an apartment for those with disabilities. I am considered to have a disability because I still have a left-side weakness from my paralysis. Because I primarily use only my right side, I had found it difficult to find a job that would support my son and me.

My daughter has since grown and started her own family. I decided to go to college and get a degree so I would not need to live in low-income housing. It takes at least six months before you actually start receiving your monthly checks after you apply for disability benefits. Subsidized housing provides a place for individuals to live while they have no income available. This is a blessing for many people.

I found many good neighbors hidden in low income. They may have looked different from others due to a disability, but they had big hearts. A lack of money and an imperfect body does not define a human being.

I believe that any person can make any place a home. This can be done by looking people in their eyes and overlooking their flaws. We have heard this message since the beginning of time. Everyone knows that beauty is indeed in the eye of the beholder.

I have never been destitute. I do not know what it would be like to live in a car. I have had to make sacrifices in my life, as we all have, and I have always been grateful for a roof over my head.

In conclusion, yes, there is a spark in low-income living.

Chapter 13

I've Learned A Few Things

L IKE ANYONE ELSE, I haven't gotten to my age without learning a thing or two. I call it gaining wisdom much like the elderly people had, when I took my first job. I don't believe that it would be possible to be so well informed about life at the age of twenty one when I first got pregnant.

The greatest gain that I've learned is that I don't have all the answers or explanations to the questions of life. I do know that I have the ability to live my life in any manner that I choose. I also know that the past is not in the present.

I can honestly state that I wish my oldest daughter was still alive. I also know that she had free will along with everyone else. If I had the ability to have forced my will on Jamie in 1988, I would most likely feel guilty because I would not have ever let her leave this world or her body. If she were alive in her body today, I wonder what her life would be like. I have learned to let go of all outcomes. I do believe that there was a purpose for her life and her death. I believe it because I feel it in my own instincts.

I have gained the knowledge that I am much stronger than I had ever imagined. I discovered that in 1994 when I woke up walking. This occurred after I woke up paralyzed. I believe that many people have untapped potential inside themselves. I do not ever want to be confined to a wheelchair again, so I've learned to take care of myself. I am responsible for my own wellbeing. I've learned that nobody is going to do it for me!

I have also chosen to be single at this time of my life. I did discover that it is wise to think about being compatible with a partner or a spouse. It is a good idea to make sure that there is more to the relationship than love. Love is a great item to have between any couple. I loved and still love all three of my children's fathers. That is a fact that I won't deny. I had discovered though, that love is not always enough even though it does not end. The fact remains that before I would ever fully commit to a marriage I would need to be clear on common goals and life styles. I did not know that would matter in 1983 when I got married. I truly believed that all our marriage would need was to love each other, we did have that love and it was disappointing when it failed. I've learned to live with disappointment too.

Getting divorced taught me to let go of wanting someone or wanting something such as marriage and family.

I've happily learned that my two living children

are amazingly resilient!   Mandy was three when she witnessed her older sister die. Today at the age of 28 she has almost gotten her doctorate in linguistics. She is a loving, and involved mother to her daughter. She is a happily married woman. She does not seem to live her life in fear or worry as I had feared she would. My son, at this time in his life does not appear to fear death as I had feared it for so many years.   It has not yet been a year since he witnessed his own Father die, yet he seems to know that his own life has a purpose and that he must move forward. I have spent much time praying for my children. I don't know who answered my prayers for their wellbeing, but I do know that I am grateful for the answered prayers. I also know that my children must decide for themselves if they choose to find their own passion in their lives. They must also make their own choices for themselves. I can't decide for anyone if they will choose to be happy or misery stricken.

I've also learned that I never stop learning. I'm not done making spiritual and mental gains. I think it would get boring if I had all the answers. I've learned to honestly embrace the mysteries of life.

I will conclude this book with a spark of unknowingness!

About The Author

K AREN WAS BORN IN Milwaukee, Wisconsin on November 4, 1962 to Denis and Patricia Higgs (nee Thimm). Since 1964 the family has lived in the house that Denis and family members built. Currently Karen is living in Watertown, Wisconsin with her son and their dog. Karen has lived in many towns and cities in Wisconsin with her children throughout the years. Currently is attending school full time until she graduates with her degree in marketing. She is a grandmother, mother, mother-in-law, and mom at this time. Her home, after many moves is now Watertown where she is currently attending school. She has one younger brother, and one older sister whom also live in Wisconsin with their families. She also has a foster brother who lived with the family for a short period in the 1970's who resides in Oklahoma with his family.

Without the constant upgrading of the medical technology this book would not be possible. Dedicated medical staff have literally saved the lives of not only Karen, but trillions of other people. The benefits for raising funds for all medical issues have showed up in all areas. The heart and brain, have, of course been favorites for Karen. Jamie had her heart surgeries done in Milwaukee, Wisconsin in a time when there was little known about severe heart defects. Karen also had her brain surgery done in Milwaukee at a time when such a location of an aneurysm in the brain would have been devastating to many. Karen wears a walk aide which is a device that electronically lifts the part of the foot that drags from previous paralysis. Her left hand has not fully come back with the fine motor skills. In her opinion, a left side weakness is a small price to pay for the reward of a life that is truly good!